# THE JOURNEY WITH GOD

## SHENEA JANUARY

# Dedication

*To every Man and Woman on a Journey with God, who has surrendered your way so that His will may be done, I dedicate this book to you.*

*Thank you for standing for the Kingdom. May His Kingdom be with you and in you forever.*

*Restore to me the joy of your salvation;*
*And make me willing to obey you.*
Psalm 51:12 (NLT)

# Contents

# Foreword

Years ago, Shenea attended my Women's Sunday school class, which was called The Woman of Excellence. Committed to learning about God and walking in His perfect will, Shenea asked many questions; such as, "How will I know?", "How do we know that we are hearing God clearly?", and "How do we know that we are on the right path or heading in the right direction?"

It is this same desire to understand and find answers that has not only supported Shenea throughout her personal experience, but also guided her in writing this devotional. Therefore, what was discovered on her own Journey, and what she shares in this book, is that God has designed for each of us, a series of experiences that takes us from knowing "about" God, to "knowing" God; from believing what God says, to trusting in Him completely.

So, as you read through these pages, I encourage you to take your time. Meditate on the Scriptures and reflections one day at a time. Let God speak to you. Recognize that the key to this "Journey" is that you are not walking alone. God is "with" you. He takes each step with you; promising never to leave or forsake you. Remember that "with God" all things are possible. You will be all He has called you to be, you will fulfill God's purpose for your life, and you will walk out your "Divine destiny."

And, although your "journey" will not look like anyone else's and your experiences may not mirror Shenea's, let the promises of God's Word, the wisdom learned, and her words of encouragement to press into God through prayer and reflection each day, inspire you to keep walking forward.

As God's Word states in Jeremiah 29:11(NLT) "For I know the plans I have for you, says the Lord, they are plans for good and not for disaster, to give you a future and a hope."

May God richly bless you as you "Journey" with Him.

***Dr. Laurel E Brown***
Evangelist, Professor, Teacher & Mentor
Riverside, California

# Acknowledgements

I would first like to thank my God for calling me and inviting me to accept this Journey with him. Secondly, THANK YOU JESUS! For guiding me through the Valley of the Shadow of Death and paying the price that I may one day be afforded this gift to walk with the Father. And, thank you to the precious Holy Spirit, for being at my side daily; constantly comforting me along the way. And to my children for being the best kids a mother could have and being on this great journey with me.

To My mother, who has never given up on me and always believed in my Journey... Thank you momma!

I would be remiss, if I did not thank my mentor, Evangelist Dr. Laurel Brown. This Woman of God was a great part of my walk in God and my journey to becoming a Women of Excellence. From Day One, she pushed me, believed in me, and saw things in me that, at the time, I could not see in myself. I will never forget the day she inspired me and told me that God said to write the things that He shows me. Well, I couldn't find the words to put to paper until after my journey with God, and He would bring those very words that she spoke to me back to my remembrance and say, "Now write". So, I am grateful to her for sowing that seed in me that would grow 12 years later. Thank you Sister Lori...

Lastly, I would like to thank my Editor, Elder Desireé Harris-Bonner, for being a Midwife the Lord used to help me to give birth to this baby. There are really no words to describe the divine connections that God places in your life along your journey. You just learn to embrace them and adore them. Woman of God, thank you for your dedication, your excellence, and the many times you have ministered to my soul during this process, so that my book baby would be healthy and delivered in the way in which it was intended... Kingdom!

To all of those who have been placed on my Journey, you all know who you are. I celebrate your Journeys with God, as we continue to work for the Kingdom.

To those who are reading this book... Thank you and may our Lord bless your soul bountifully!

# Introduction

I have spent many of the early years of my salvation wondering, *who am I*? Through the years, I would often hear some of my spiritual 'Mothers in the Faith', like Ambassador Juanita Bynum or Pastor Sheryl Brady, teach that to walk in your purpose and experience the fullness of God, you have to know who you are and walk in the authentic you.

I believed that because I was a realist, I *was* being authentic and true to who I was. Little did I know that it had nothing to do with walking in the authentic me, nor understanding my identity in the Kingdom... Thus, my prayers were, "Lord, WHO AM I?"

Well, June 27, 2013 started the journey when I would begin to find out. I lost my business, and in less than 3 months (within the blink of an eye), I began to hit rock bottom. I thought I had done something wrong; that I had offended God.

I didn't know it would cost me all that I knew.

Jesus said, *"For whoever wants to save his life will lose it, but whoever loses his life for me will find it. What good will it be for a man if he gains the whole world, yet forfeits his soul? Or what can a man give in exchange for his soul?"* ~Matthew 16:25-26

What I had discovered about life up to this point would be nothing compared to the journey that was ahead of me; a Journey of discovering the authentic me and a journey of a lifetime with the Lover of my soul.

So, in the pages to follow, I will share with you some of the lessons I've learned, and the seasons you will experience.

*Shenea January*

# DAY 1

## The Journey...

*"For those God foreknew he also predestined to be conformed to the image of his Son, that he might be the firstborn among many brothers and sisters. And those he predestined, he also called; those he called, he also justified; those he justified, he also glorified."*

~Romans 8:29-30

*The Journey* is a walk with God. It is why Jesus came and paid the price for you and me… that one day you will have that connection back to God. *The Journey* is when God calls the *Authentic YOU* (the place inside you where God dwells, in your SOUL) and you answer the call.

When you answer the call the birthing process begins. It is now that your journey will start to prepare you to give birth to your God-given purpose.

Yes, you will have to go through the wilderness, as did Christ. You will go through many deserts and valleys; however, if your heart's desire is, *not my will, but Father Thy will be done*. You will see the salvation of the Lord.

The Journey is all about the Kingdom of God and He wants to reveal it to you. You have a purpose, and in order to walk in it authentically, you have to know who you are… and you don't know who you are, until you walk with the person who created you.

God!

So have you answered the call yet? Or do you hear Him calling?

On this journey, you will lose something, because you are dying to your old man and being born again into your *Authentic You*; who you are in the Kingdom of God.

It's a Journey of a lifetime!

## JOURNEY LESSON

*I discovered that the Journey was one of the greatest gifts to Mankind. This journey cost me a lot of pain. For 40 years, I did what I wanted to do and now I was being called to walk in my purpose. No man knows the hour in which their true journey will begin, but there is no doubt that you will feel it when it arrives. The Authentic You will be awakened and you will soon die to self in order to give birth in the Spirit. Be encouraged, because of this you can be assured: God will be with you every step of the Way.*

*When God first called me I did not know what was happening, all I knew was that I wanted more and I had lost everything I had nothing to lose. I was tired of living life as usual and desperately desired truth in my inner most being.*

*I had a choice to remain the same, or to go down a path that was dark, with no idea where it would lead. All I had was a thought deep inside wooing me to turn down the path of the unknown. It was an invitation from God inviting me to walk with Him and He has been faithful through it all.*

***I will lead the blind by ways they have not known, along unfamiliar paths I will guide them; I will turn the darkness into light before them and make the rough places smooth. These are the things I will do; I will not forsake them.*** *~Isaiah 42:16*

# DAY 2

## Grace is on the Path

*"Let us then with confidence draw near to the throne of grace, that we may receive mercy and find grace to help in time of need."*

~Hebrews 4:16

Grace is the first of many gifts that will show up on the path of your journey. This is God's sign that He will never leave you nor forsake you.

Your *Authentic you* knows this Grace and from the very beginning understands that no matter what happens, God has you, and you must trust Him without knowing what's to come. You will have a sense of comfort that most people will not understand.

You may not even understand it!

Yet, always remember... this is your *Journey with God* and only He knows the purpose.

God told Paul "**My grace is sufficient for you, for my power is made perfect in weakness.**" (2 Cor. 12:9)

It's important to receive the Grace of God during your journey. In fact, you will not be able to move to the next level until you do. This Grace will have you to surrender because the Authentic you is being taught to submit to the process; the Kingdom process. With all the Journey Lessons, you will need Grace like never before, and will notice that it shows up every time.

This Grace allows you to come boldly to the throne of God and ask for what you need to get through the Journey... and the Father is waiting to bless you with it.

Grace is what this journey is all about and this grace will bless your soul.

## JOURNEY LESSON

*When I started my journey, I lost almost everything I owned. My life was changed in a blink of an eye. I hit rock bottom. I didn't know how my children and I were going to survive. I mean rock bottom!*

*I remember wanting to run and make things happen, because I was tired of just sitting; thinking that I should be doing something. I remember God saying, "Who are you running to? If you run, you will only be running from yourself." He then said, "I'm extending grace to you. If you can't receive it from Me, you will not be able to receive it from anyone, not even your husband.*

*I often asked God was I being rebuked, or did I do something wrong to offend him? His answer was, "You asked for this."*

*It was then brought back to my remembrance the prayer that I often prayed," God, please motivate me. I'm tired, so if you don't do it, it won't be done."*

*How could losing everything motivate me?*

*Well, it taught me to walk with God, trust and receive His Grace in this wilderness place, where He was my only motivation. The Grace of God in that season was more than I could even think or imagine.*

# DAY 3

---

# When Vision is Obstructed

*"...but when he opened his eyes he could see nothing. So they led him by the hand into Damascus. For three days he was blind."*

~Acts 9:8

When your Journey begins, you will come to understand the road is narrow. It's narrow because the only thing you can trust is the NOW and totally relying on God's leading.

You will be blinded at times.

The reason this happens is because you can no longer rely on the path that you once walked. The blindness teaches us to acknowledge God in all of our ways; to not depend on our former ways and trust that He will make our path straight (**Proverb 3:6**).

Paul was a great witness to this. Along his Journey, he too was blinded in order to submit to Christ, that it would lead him one day to the Father. You are being prepared to be a witness of the Kingdom of God, and in order for this to happen, you will also have to submit to Christ's instructions.

This path may seem lonely. However, God is always with you, even when you can't see him. I encourage you to keep your eyes on the path He sets before you... Even when the path seems long and you can't see the end.

Know that your destination is predestined and there is an end to everything.

Trust that which was started in you will be completed until the day of Christ Jesus! (**Philippians 1:6**)

Trust the correction to your vision. When you see through the lens of Christ, you are graced with the ability to believe what you see in the Spirit is possible. If you take them off, you will see as the world and believe what you see is impossible.

*"Jesus looked at them and said, "With man this is impossible, but with God all things are possible"*

(Matthew 19:26)

God's Word will be true to you if you believe.

Even though God will not show you the end of the journey, you will have a peace that He has you, and your faith will carry you through to the *Authentic YOU.*

## JOURNEY LESSON

*In the beginning of my journey I was blinded and could not see. This was another fear for me, as I was always able to discern the times spiritually, or knew how to make a business decision naturally. However, nothing I tried worked and I could not see what God was doing.*

*I later learned that this happens in order to get you to trust in God; no matter what it looks like. I had to believe, with everything in me, that in making the decision to follow Christ completely, God would not let me fall. And always remembering the promise He gave me: I WILL NOT FAIL THEE...*

*I've come to relate to a blind person and understand the two circumstances of NEVER being able to see, and ONCE being able to see.*

*For a person blinded at birth, fear is a little different, being that they have never seen danger. If a truck blew his horn, it sounds big, but they can't truly fathom how big it really is to know that it's dangerous.*

*The visual of a big pit-bull that barks... they would not know that the breed of such a dog was dangerous. Now, a person that was once able to see, if they heard a truck horn their first thought would be to get out of the way, knowing it may be hard for the truck to stop. The pit-bull, they know what it looks like and the outcome if it were to get ahold of them.*

*It is the same way in the Spirit. Once you are able to see and hear in the Spirit and then are blinded, it is very fearful. But in this case, it is a blessing in disguise. In order for you to walk in the Authentic YOU, you're blinded, so your sight can become one with the Creator.*

# DAY 4

## Be Still...

*"Be still, and know that I am God; I will be exalted among the nations, I will be exalted in the earth."*

~Psalm 46:10

God can't give us instructions if we are always trying to make it happen or make sense out of a situation.

Being still is a skill that everyone must learn on their journey. It is your defense as the enemy puts distractions on your path. You must not only learn this skill, but use it often.

Being still does not mean to just sit in a position and not move. It means to quiet your mind and stop your thoughts from running rampant. Our human nature will always try to figure things out and on this *Journey with God,* it will do this more than ever. The enemy knows that God is protecting your soul. So, he will try to confuse you with thoughts that will disturb your peace and stop your process.

Once your peace is disrupted, it's hard to connect with God. This trick the enemy knows all too well.

Being still is a weapon the Lord gives us to fight off the enemy. Remember "For we wrestle not against flesh and blood, but against principalities, against powers, against the ruler s of the darkness of this world, against spiritual wickedness in high places."

Never forget, you are more than a conqueror! There is a blessing in this lesson if you obey. It is not up to us to understand why God is asking us to be still; it will be revealed in HIS timing. In the meantime, bless and praise HIM, for the battle is not yours, but the Lord's...

## JOURNEY LESSON

*Although being still is tough, I've learned that if I had not learned this important lesson, I would not be on the path I'm on today. For many years I had heard the Lord say, "Be still." I was quite frustrated, because I thought I had already learned this lesson.*

*Apparently not!*

*So, one day I asked the Lord, "Why do You keep telling me to be still? I thought I had passed this test!" Once again, He said, "Be still and know that I am God." I finally understood what was being asked of me. In learning this, it taught me how to survive in the Valley of the Shadow of Death; by learning how to listen in the spirit, and more than anything, see in the spirit.*

*This lesson also taught me the difference of roads vs. Journeys. Roads are set to distract you, but Journeys are meant to lead you to the path of righteous for His name sake (the destination).*

*It also taught me to see the giants in the land, the roadblocks that were set to stop me. I was able to see the Lord fighting for me, which showed the greatness in me.*

# DAY 5

# Forgiveness Clears the Path

*"He restores my soul; He guides me in the paths of righteousness For His name's sake."*

~Psalm 23:3

When you answer the call of God, there are many things you should be clear of, as you start your journey.

One of the first, and greatest, lessons you will have to address on your journey is Forgiveness to others and to yourself... When you are open to forgive, The Holy Spirit will then show you the truth of the matter; helping you to realize your part in it and what it is producing in you.

The *bad* of whatever the situation is, still has some *good*. Forgiveness allows you to see it... Once you forgive others, it is important to forgive yourself. God lives in each one of us, so when you don't forgive yourself, you work against God; stunting your own growth.

Forgiveness allows God to go deeper inside you to the core of your soul and clean you up so that your journey will get you to your destination.

Hear this! Forgiveness is another weapon that God gives you to fight the enemy on your journey. The enemy knows that if you don't forgive, your sins will not be forgiven and he will keep you bound to the roadblock called "hardening of the heart".

Betty Wright said it this way, "If you learn the secret of how to forgive, a better and a longer life you'll live."

Loved ones, forgiveness is a gift from God.

*"If you forgive those who sin against you, your heavenly Father will forgive you."*
~ Matthew 6:14

## JOURNEY LESSON

*At the onset of my journey, I must say, I was a little angry at where I was… and the enemy did a good job of making it appear as if my family and others I thought were for me, couldn't care less about me. I first believed I had a right to be angry because I supported everyone else, I took really good care of my staff, I have always been there for my children, and so on.*

*Surely they would be there for me! Before this part of my journey started, I had the privilege of a 9 month journey with the Lord, taking pictures of the sunrise or the sunset and nature. From each picture, the Lord would give me an understanding of the Word. This particular day, as the sun was setting, this came to me. "…Don't sin by letting anger control you. Don't let the sun go down while you are still angry."*

*I never understood why I was able to forgive others for long periods of time. Sure, I was mad for a moment, but if I saw them a year later, I was able to embrace them like it never happened. It wasn't important! It took far more energy out of me to hold on to their offense.*

*My **Journey with God** reaffirmed to me that forgiveness is Mandatory. So, forgive lest you not be forgiven…*

# DAY 6

---

# Seek God with all Your Heart

*"Then you will call upon Me and come and pray to Me, and I will listen to you. You will seek Me and find Me when you search for Me with all your heart…"*

~Jeremiah 29:12-13

This Journey is with God. He wants to reveal to you things about Himself that you have not yet known. This is not something someone can teach you. My Lord, this is an experience with the Almighty God; the Alpha and the Omega, the beginning and the End!

Oftentimes, we can get confused when God continues to tell us to seek Him. We think because we read our Word, we go to church, and we pray and so on, that we are seeking Him... Seeking God is much more than that.

God wants to walk *with* you; and how can two walk together unless they agree? When you are in a relationship, you spend time with that person, asking questions and getting to know their heart.

Well, the Lord wants to show you His Glory and for that my friends, you will have to seek Him and call upon Him. When you desire to understand His heart, you will find His Grace... and when you find Grace, you will see His face.

Matthew 7:7 *says, "Ask and it will be given to you, seek and you will find; knock and the door will be open to you"...* Don't limit where you seek God. It can be looking at a beautiful rose in the backyard and He will reveal a truth to you about your life or His kingdom. He may place one word on your heart that will not go away. Google, research the word, you will be surprised as you end up right where He wanted you to be; revealing what it is He wants you to know. Remember, the true things of God are always revealed to you.

## JOURNEY LESSON

*I can often remember, along the journey, the Lord telling me to seek Him. And it was frustrating at first, because I thought that I was seeking Him... I finally asked God, "Why do you keep saying seek me?*

*You see, God wants us to ask Him questions. It is when you ask, that it will be given unto you. So, I noticed that as words or thoughts came to my heart, I would be inspired to Google it. I was amazed at what I would come across. God would lead me to the answer of what I had been seeking Him for in prayer; questions I had in my heart that I wouldn't say out loud, leaving me in awe every time.*

*There are mysteries that he shows you when you seek Him. These mysteries will help you along your journey to reach your destination. It is imperative that you understand what God wants to reveal to you, because there are truths that only He can show you... only He can answer. Remember, you are on a journey with God and you must seek Him until seeking Him becomes first nature!*

**"One thing I ask from the LORD, this only do I seek: that I may dwell in the house of the LORD all the days of my life, to gaze on the beauty of the LORD and to seek him in his temple."** ~Psalm 27:4

# DAY 7

## Denying Yourself

*"Then Jesus said to His disciples, "If anyone wishes to come after Me, he must deny himself, and take up his cross and follow Me. For whoever wishes to save his life will lose it; but whoever loses his life for My sake will find it"*

*~Matthew 16:24-25*

If you have found yourself challenged by losing a job, your health, a relationship, or your business... know that it was not to hurt you, but will be used as a tool to heal you, so that your authentic self can be revealed to you.

Along the Journey of Life, when you come to the crossroads of understanding who you really are, the *Authentic You* is who you truly are in God. Your earthly knowledge will not be invited into this realm. You will have to be willing to lose the knowledge of who you are on earth, to understand who you are in the Kingdom.

There is a vast difference...

The *Authentic You* is the core of you, which is your spirit. It is the very part of you that the Lord made in His image. Therefore, in order to walk with God, we have to be willing to pick up our cross and follow Christ and renew our minds to understand Kingdom truths.

This means that you have to forsake all others, in order for Him to lead the way to the Father. Family and friends may mean well and love you. But, as you're being prepared to experience the Grace of God in your life, He does not want you contaminated with the advice or guidance that friends and loved ones will try to offer. Their understanding is of this world and God wants to reveal the understanding of His Kingdom.

*"No eye has seen, no ear has heard, no mind has conceived what God has prepared for those who love him but God has revealed it to us by his Spirit"* ~1 Cor 2:9-10

## JOURNEY LESSON

*I did not understand in the beginning of my journey why everything was taken from me. One moment I had it all, and in a second, I had lost it all. My family did not understand it either, and friends fell by the wayside.*

*It was hard for me to comprehend, because I thought I had done something wrong. Nonetheless, I made a choice and decided to trust God, even though I had no idea what was ahead. If I was going to get this right, I knew deep down in my soul that I would have to capitulate my will, that God's will could be done.*

*I made up my mind and settled the matter in my heart that I was going to follow Christ. I wanted an experience with God more than ever in my life and I was willing to let it all go...*

# DAY 8

---

# Natural vs Spiritual Birth

*"The Spirit of the LORD will rest on him-- the Spirit of wisdom and of understanding, the Spirit of counsel and of might, the Spirit of the knowledge and fear of the LORD."*
~Isaiah 11:2

At conception in the Spirit, it will require your *Yes*... Once you make the decision that you want to walk with God, THEN HE will begin to knit your purpose together inside you, much like pregnancy.

When a woman is first impregnated, she is faced with the decision to give birth to her baby or to abort. As Children of God we all know that aborting is not an option; however, it is still a choice that will be yours to make and the outcome will be with you and God...

The normal term for women to carry a baby is 40 weeks. There are 3 trimesters that she will go through, and each is needed in order to develop the baby for the life it will live out of the womb. You may read about the process, listen to doctors or other moms share with you what to expect and what's to come, yet the outcome of your pregnancy and birth will still be the Creator and yours alone. The only other person who knows what will truly take place in your womb is God, as He knits the new life (purpose) together, preparing you and your baby for what's to come.

No one can tell for certain what the baby is going to look like, but with expectancy you await its arrival.

*We all will come to this crossroad: to choose to give birth to our God-given Purpose or to abort it during the process. When this choice knocked at my door, I was at a point in life, where I was tired of questioning the gifts that God had placed in me. Without knowing what would follow, I made the decision not to question God again; I would believe what He showed me; I wanted to truly walk in the purpose of who I had been allowed on this earth to be... I wanted to live life. The only problem was, I didn't know how.*

*So, in order for me to know, I needed to surrender to God's will and make the conscious decision to let the God in me, reveal the Authentic ME!*

*I learned that there was a process I had to go through, which was much like being pregnant with child naturally.*

*These were the stages:*

1.  ***The Call (Prerequisite)** – Something happens that creates a loud sound in your life. This was also the prerequisite stage before beginning your journey.*

2.  ***The Process (The Journey)** - I was given the choice. The choice was to do things my way or trust God; to trust Him with no understanding of what I*

*was to experience. Such as a young mother being pregnant for the first time, not knowing all that her next 9 months would be...*

3.  ***Labor*-** I was tired often and experienced a lot of travailing in the spirit.

### *BIRTH!*

# DAY 9

## Understanding His Ways

*"For as the heavens are higher than the earth, so are my ways higher than your ways and my thoughts than your thoughts."*

*~Isaiah 55:9 NASB*

The journey is all about your coming into the person God created you to be. The Spiritual you, the Authentic YOU! While on this path, everything else has to die. Religion, tradition, superstitions, your will; everything that exalts itself above the name of Jesus!

While these things serve some good, it will not get you to your destination.

The journey is about truly understanding the Love of God...realizing that you are blessed with Life and to enjoy it! But wait, there is more! Jesus said that we would do greater things than He did, because He goes to the Father. Are you doing greater things? Do you know the gifts that God has given you to do those greater things? Have you been on the journey "going through" and seen God literally move everything out of your way to protect you? As psalm 91 says, have you seen your angels commanded to keep you from a situation? Have you seen God put His Wings around you?

Beloved, this is what the journey is about, to fully experience the Word of God made alive in your life. Allow God to make Himself known to you in ways you never imagined.

## JOURNEY LESSON

*This is the part of the journey where I had no choice, except to let go, because in trying to understand it, it just did not make sense! In these times of frustration, the Word of God that would come to my heart:* **lean not to your own understanding.**

*God wants to demonstrate Himself to us. When we allow Him to do so, He blesses us with a knowledge that is not of this world and leads us to wisdom.*

*"Trust in the Lord with all your heart, and do not trust in your own understanding. Acknowledge Him in all your ways, and He will make your paths straight".*

~Proverbs 3:5-6

*"Therefore let us move beyond the elementary teachings about Christ and be taken forward to maturity, not laying again the foundation of repentance from acts that lead to death, and of faith in God.*

~Hebrew 6:1

# DAY 10

## Can't Trace Him... Trust Him

*"...because God has said, 'Never will I leave you; never will I forsake you."*

~Hebrews 13:15

Abraham left his family at 75 years old, to set out on a journey, because God told him to. At his old age, he trusted God and believed the promises. Along his journey, God showed Abraham new promises, but there was still adversity along the way... yet, this adversity opened the door for the promises.

When God instructs you to get up and move along your journey, it's for a greater purpose. He will always make a promise to you. Know that He will not fail you and He is faithful to fulfill it. You have everything you need to finish the race and that which you don't have, trust that God is providing and commanding it on your path. He is not like us, He doesn't get sidetracked. He is an on-time GOD.

Yes!

You may have to take a break to rest, and the resting point may be in a dry place; however, know that's not your destination. Ask God for traveling grace and keep moving. The promise is yet ahead.

## JOURNEY LESSON

*One of the prayers I often prayed was, "Lord, I don't want to be like Moses and the Children of Israel, going around the mountain for 40 years, while the promises were right in front of them."*

*Wow, I could visualize it.*

*I could see why they were scared. Nevertheless, I realized that it would be a huge misstep for me, if I knew how the story ended for them, yet did not trust God for myself. So, I was convinced that if that was going to be my lot, then I'd better start trusting God in every area of my life.*

# DAY 11

## His Peace Will Keep You

*"You will keep him in perfect peace, whose mind is stayed on you: Because he trusts in you."*

~Isaiah 26:3

Our mind is consumed with information almost 24 hours a day. If you allow your mind to control you, it will always take you off the path. Why? Because the cares of the world will consume you and the enemy's plan is to divert you from your path. Therefore, finding and keeping peace on your journey is something you must do.

It is the peace of God that will allow you to go within and find rest for your soul when the world around you is turned upside down. God dwells inside of you and wants to commune with the Authentic You!

God dwells in your heart and the journey is all about God dealing with your heart. While He is doing so, trust He will protect it. The enemy will fight you for your peace, so be aware, but do not be afraid. Just as Jesus reminded the disciples, let this also be a reminder to you:

*"Peace I leave with you; My peace I give to you.*
*I do not give to you as the world gives. Do not*
*let your hearts be troubled; do not be afraid"*
(John 14:27)

When you find yourself losing your peace, go back to one of the first weapons we talked about and that is, BE STILL. Remember, meditation grounds your peace, and in your stillness, think of the goodness of God and all that He has done for you.

## JOURNEY LESSON

*I always refer to the beginning of my journey, because it was the place where it all began and each process was learned. It was the beginning of the new me being awakened and the most important part of my walk with God. In this season of transition, I was forced to be still.*

*At the time, I did not understand how being still could or would better my situation. I was homeless and felt like such a failure! My business wasn't growing, and I couldn't seem to come up with a plan that would work. Those around me asked questions like, "Why don't you just get a job and change your situation, so that you can get back on track and live the way you were?"*

*But that was it! I did not want to live the life I had lived before; living for the world, yet no step closer to knowing who I was. I understood that I could not live life as usual and that I was going to have to turn and truly trust God, and in return He would give me the peace that surpasses all understanding...*

*Initially, finding peace for me was difficult; however, it was also the greatest thing I would ever learn to do. There is no doubt in my mind that the enemy was after my mind. But, it was even clearer to me that the Lord was giving me grace to renew my mind.*

# DAY 12

## Know what Season You're in

*"To everything there is a season, and a time to every purpose under the heaven."*

~Ecclesiastes 3:1 KJV

Seasons will change right before your eyes. If you are not paying attention, how do you know how to govern yourself? While on your journey to discovering the *Authentic YOU*, knowing which season you're in is important. The natural Seasons serve as a sign of the same Seasons that takes place in the Spirit.

As the Seasons change, they are a compass for you to stay on the right path or to make the proper adjustment for the change that is taking place.

Once you are aware of the seasons in your life, when they come back around, you will understand what time it is, and get through the season much wiser.


## JOURNEY LESSON

*For nine months I had the privilege of going on a journey with God and taking photos throughout the land. I had passed down this street every day; the trees were beautiful, in season, and I marveled at God's creation.*

*Well, the season began changing and I had stopped paying attention. God said, "Look at the trees. They have no leaves on them." I remember thinking, Wow! I have been so busy with life; I really did not pay attention. They are all gone! He told me the seasons had changed right before my eyes. He then asked me, "Can you find the beauty in the trees now?"*

*After carefully observing the tree, I was in awe that even though the tree was barren, it was the most beautiful sight to see. He said, "Pay attention to the Seasons."*

*I did not know these would be the very words that would come along, later in my journey, to help me understand the season I was in. One day, while I was feeling sorry for myself, I was thinking, "like, what is happening with my life right now?" And the Holy Spirit brought this to my remembrance, "Remember the season of the trees not bearing fruit?"*

*"Yes..."*

*He said, "Such is the season you're in now. Can you find the beauty in it? I was in awe and at great peace. Although my life felt like it was not going anywhere, I understood that it was winter for me and a season for rest.*

*God is always trying to communicate with us. This is a journey **with** Him, not just a journey **to** him. Know what season you are in and God will continue to direct your steps. If I had not learned this very important lesson in that season of my life, I would have become weary along my journey.*

*Know your Seasons... Here are some signs of the seasons spiritually. From this day forward, pray to God about each one; He will make known to you each season in your life, so that you may stay on the path He has set before you.*

**SPRING:** *Discovering what life is about as a believer.*

You will notice a new thirst and awareness for more of God. Excitement of what your faith can become; like hearing birds chirping after a long winter.

**SUMMER:** *Satisfaction in God's love, joy and peace.*

You will notice a passion to belong and grow, filled with abundance and discovery of how God can use you; feeling God's presence regularly, with a strong desire to share your faith.

**AUTUMN:** *A sense of weariness.*

This is a time of transition. Harvesting the growth of summer (your strengths and gifts) and using it to help others grow (bear fruit).

**WINTER:** *A time for rest.*

This is when God feels far away and/or it seems that you can't see or notice anything happening; there is a sense of being stuck and your faith may feel dormant.

# DAY 13

---

# Roadblocks along the Path

*"Yet he saved them for his name's sake, that he might make known his mighty power. He rebuked the Red Sea, and it became dry, and he led them through the deep as through a desert. So he saved them from the hand of the foe and redeemed them from the power of the enemy."*

~Psalm 106:8-10

At times, the Journey may feel long, and you're thinking, "Lord, will I ever get there? There are so many obstacles!" And, you may be thinking about the clock ticking, and the delusion of it running out of time on you, grips you with fear. The enemy will put all kinds of roadblocks in your way, because he knows you're tired (fatigued in the spirit).

He did the same thing to Jesus in the wilderness.

Although these feelings are real, see them as determents to try and stop you. These ROADBLOCKS are old tricks he has used from the beginning. See, when you begin to look at 'Time', you'll start viewing things as the world does; allowing panic to kick in, which prompts you to operate from the fleshly realm (in your feelings).

Allow me to encourage you in the Lord this day. God is faithful and Time, as we know it, is not the same Time as our Father knows it. There is nothing under the sun that our father is unaware of.

The children of Israel saw the sea as a roadblock. They assumed Moses had led them to the desert to die. We now know that this was not reality.

When you see a roadblock in the natural, you see them as signs of protection, so that you will not get stuck. When you see the roadblocks on your *Journey with God*, recognize that they serve the same purpose, but in the spirit. See them as signs the Lord is putting on your path so that you can overcome them.

## JOURNEY LESSON

*There were times on my journey when I thought I was going to lose my mind. Yes, I said it, because it's the truth, and if I'm going to encourage you along your journey, then I have to keep it real!*

*There were times I did not know how I was going to feed my children. I could not tell them or NO one else of this, because I did not want my kids to panic or worry, and I did not want others to think that I was unfit or losing it. So, the only place I had to turn was to God from 2am to 6am in the morning. Yes, there were long nights. But, I see it this way. It was in the WEE hours of the night, that He walked with me and talked with me and let me know that it was going to work out... just trust Him. It was during those hours that my Angels were at war with the enemy, defeating my battle, because I was crying out to God.*

*Before Sunrise, God already had things worked out. This testimony is just one of many that I had to face on my journey.*

# DAY 14

## What does the Lord Require of You?

*"He has made it clear to you, mortal man, what is good and what the LORD is requiring from you— to act with justice, to treasure the LORD's gracious love, and to walk humbly in the company of your God."*

~Micah 6:8

There are paths predestined for your journey. These paths tug at your soul and you feel them, but sometimes the obstacles on our path detour us. The Lord already knows these things, which is why He also used those in the Bible to write, so that they could inspire you along your journey; just as you also have a huge role to do for the Kingdom.

So what does the Lord require of us? To follow the ways set before us. Jesus walked the earth just as you and I. He knows every situation that will arise and has left us the map to stay on the right path. There were others that were chosen after Him to Journey and teach us about the paths, so that when we are discouraged along the way, the inspired Word of God will direct us to the right paths. God has taught you, oh mortal man, the way.

*"Thus said the Lord "Stand by the ways and see and ask for the ancient paths, where the good way is and walk in it; and you will find rest for your souls." ~Jeremiah 6:16*

The Journey takes us from glory to glory, so some things along your path, you have already lived and seen the light on, and it will come up again to bring you higher when discovering the *Authentic You.*

## JOURNEY LESSON

*I questioned myself along my journey a lot. God was leading me and directing me, yet at times because it was not going the way I thought it should, I second-guessed myself.*

*God is faithful, and if there is one thing I understood, it was that this journey is with Him and that He is directing my path. That wasn't the problem though. I trusted God but I did not trust me. So, this is the area where God worked the most with me; because in order for me to walk in my authentic self, I must be able to trust the God in me that spoke to me. Then I could be certain of what was required of me.*

*There were many times that all I had was a Word, and if I followed the word that was on my heart by searching it out in the bible or even googling it for meaning, the Holy Spirit would lead me right to what God wanted me to know and understand. This season was the best! I came to understand that God will move heaven and earth to make sure that we understand which way we should go.*

*My part was to stay connected to God, and when I veered off the path, everything in my core (the Authentic me), told me that I was off course. This happened so that I could learn to walk humbly with my God. This is what the journey my friends is all about.*

# DAY 15

## Gratitude Determines Attitude

*"In everything give thanks: for this is the will of God in Christ Jesus concerning you."*

~1 Thessalonians 5:18

Know that gratitude along your journey is everything! It draws the presence of God into your atmosphere. Daily, find the good in any bad situation, because this is the will of God for you. When you learn to find the good in the bad, then you learn to be more like Christ. This allows the Lord to use you for Kingdom purposes. It moves you from glory to glory!

Gratitude in all things allows the Grace of God to move in extraordinary ways. Gratitude allows the Grace to take you higher in the knowledge of the Kingdom of God. That is also God's will for you, so the *Authentic You* can remember who you are in the Kingdom and the purpose for which you have been called; that you may be a vessel on earth that the Lord can use to bring glory to His name. So that others may know Christ and the power of His suffering.

Lastly, when you're grateful for what you have, more will be given. I know you're saying "I have been patient, not complaining, I've been grateful. When will more be given?" My answer would be, that's the wrong attitude my friend. Keep a good attitude until God changes your altitude; let this be your focus, and stay in the Spirit of gratitude. It will lift you in due season. When life pulls at your heart, close your eyes and say this:

*"My life isn't perfect, but I am GRATEFUL..."*

## JOURNEY LESSON

*When the Journey began, I initially looked at the bad in my situation and couldn't see the good. But the Lord taught me the importance of being grateful in everything.*

*At first, I didn't understand what He was doing; I just knew the wisdom that I previously had didn't mean much in this season. However, I noticed later along my journey, that this became second nature to me. To the point where others thought I was not being realistic.*

*For example: When I lived in the back of my office, there was no shower. So, in my attempt to be sophisticated, I came up with a great idea. I searched online for portable tubs or showers and found some! But the prices were out of my budget at the time and so purchasing one was not an option. Then the Lord, with His gracious self, dropped this in my spirit – Get one of the largest plastic containers they sell at Walmart. I could fill it up and make bath water.*

*He reminded me of many homeless individuals, who would purchase an inexpensive gym membership, just to be able to take a shower. Laughing, I thought this was so simple! From that moment forward, each time I took a bath in my plastic Walmart container, all I could do was thank God for hot water and the means to take a bath.*

*Be thankful in all things...*

# DAY 16

## You are an Heir...

*"For His spirit joins with our spirit to affirm that we are God's children. And since we are His children we are His heirs. In fact, together with Christ we are heirs of God's glory. But if we are to share His glory, we must also share His suffering."*

~Romans 8:16-17

The *Authentic You* is who God created you to be. When you walk in who you were created to be, you become a witness along with the Spirit of God and the kingdom of heaven. You become a child of the promise. When you truly understand who you are, then you will be able to receive the gift of Grace. This Grace allows you to walk with God and to commune with Him as Christ did. It allows you to understand the Kingdom and your purpose in which you have been called, as Christ did. It is a journey of a life time! And it is Gods pleasure to walk with you, once walking with Him you can never go back to being the same.

So if you have asked God WHO are you or to SHOW you who you are, then know that the Journey is set to show you. It is God's desire that you understand along your journey truly who you are and the one who created you.

God takes pleasure in walking with you; and being so personal with you, that you will never be the same. When God changed the general's names in the Bible, it was because they had finally understood who they were. They had been tried in the fire and survived. They never gave up. Instead, they trusted and believed God, despite what it looked like, and God showed them his glory.

Beloved, you are an heir, together with Christ, of God's Glory. The Journey is not to take *from* you; it is to *give* you your birth right. The Journey is a gift from God, and although it will be painful at times, where there is no PAIN... there is no GAIN.

## JOURNEY LESSON

*What I loved most about my Journey with God was the constant revelation of the Kingdom; the understanding of the deeper reason for why Christ came, that one day I would understand the Authentic me and accept the invitation to walk with my God. To receive the Grace that the apostle Paul so greatly spoke of that was to come.*

*I was also saddened, because I understood that many of my peers and leaders have never be on this journey with God; therefore, never really comprehending who they are, but walking in tradition as to what they had been taught.*

*I always thought my ministry was to the world and my purpose was to share the good news to bring others to Christ, to open the blind eyes that they may see, and their deaf ears that they may hear. What I learned along my journey was that my purpose was more for the Church; to those who were already believers of Christ, yet asleep.*

*Everyone wants to be an heir of the glory, but not an heir of the suffering. You cannot truly live for the Kingdom, unless you are willing to die to the ways of this world. There is a cost associated with surrendering, but remember this, "And after you have suffered a little while, the God of all grace, who has called you to his eternal glory in Christ, will himself restore, confirm, strengthen, and establish you." ~1 Peter 5:10*

# DAY 17

## Wisdom Calls

*"I love those who love me, and those who seek me diligently find me."*

~Proverb 8:17 NKJV

The Journey is a call from God and everyone must choose to answer it. This call is not the same call as the beginning of salvation. This call is to know and walk in who you were destined to be.

When you set it in your heart to say 'Yes' to the call of God, He assigns the first of His works to you, and this awakens the Authentic YOU to truly understand a wisdom in God you have never known. This call is the "deep calling unto deep"; The Lord calling to deeper things in you. The *Authentic You!* This is new. You have never experienced it before, so don't try to bring what you thought you knew, because it is not invited. The Lord says, *"Behold I will do a new thing."* (Isaiah 43:10)

Wisdom is a friend of God, and on your journey, it will be a friend to you; perhaps, the only one you will have as you are walking with God. Before the world began, God loved Wisdom, as Wisdom was the craftsman at His side.

And God loves you.

So, if you seek God in a way like never before, you will find Him in a way like never before.

> *"I was filled with delight day after day,*
> *Rejoicing always in his presence, rejoicing in his*
> *whole world and delighting in mankind."*
> ~Proverbs 8:22-23

## JOURNEY LESSON

*The Love, Wisdom, Grace, and Understanding that I experienced from God on the Journey to discovering the Authentic Me, was like nothing I had ever experienced or heard anyone speak about. This is why it was fearful in the beginning, because there was no one I could speak within my circle, who understood what I was going through.*

*The Lord would later explain that He did not want me to be contaminated with any other wisdom, than the wisdom He was teaching me in that season.*

*I had attended a wonderful church, been taught by great leaders, schools books, etc.; however, this was different, and I understood that God was going to be the one to teach me from this point on. Teach me Kingdom truths!*

*The Lord dropped this scripture in my spirit, many years ago: "See, the former things have taken place, and I'm announcing the new things— before they spring into being I'm telling you about them." ~Isaiah 42:9. ISV*

*This is the new thing that God is doing in this time; calling those to their Kingdom position. The alarm has sounded and Wisdom has made her call.*

*Will you answer?*

# DAY 18

## Detours on the Highway

*"The LORD says, "I will guide you along the best pathway for your life. I will advise you and watch over you."*

~Psalm 32:8

Everything you experience in the natural has a spiritual meaning that directs you on the path God has set before you on your journey. Many times, we forget that what God is doing is a new thing, and our minds can become stuck, causing tunnel vision.

Detours happen to set you back on the right course and to keep your mentality constantly transforming toward the Kingdom, so that it does not revert to the pattern of this world; your old way of doing things.

*Do not conform to the pattern of this world, but be transformed by the renewing of your mind. Then you will be able to test and approve what God's will is—his good, pleasing and perfect will.* **Romans 12:2**

Your Journey is directing you to your God-given purpose, and the only way to get there is to give up your will, that His will may be done. It isn't that your plans were not awesome! It's that God's plans are always greater. We serve a God who created the world, the universe, and everything in it; therefore, He knows the best path to get us to our destination.

*And a highway will be there; it will be called the Way of Holiness; it will be for those who walk on that Way. The unclean will not journey on it; wicked fools will not go about on it. ~Isaiah 35:8*

## JOURNEY LESSON

*There are many roads along the Journey with God. And there are detours set along your path by God. A lot of times, we think it's because we've done something wrong, and you will begin to criticize yourself and your choices. But be encouraged today, and know that some detours are the Lord's doing. There is nothing that you have done or can do about it, except to embrace them.*

*A dear friend of mine was in town for a conference, in which she was a participant. This was her first time in California, and in her downtime, she wanted to visit family who lived about an hour from my home.*

*On our way back, I took the usual route; however, about 20 minutes from home, there was some roadwork on the freeway that forced us to detour. I tried everything to avoid it. Not only could I not avoid it, but there were 3 more detours, causing us to take 2 hours to get home. Go figure!*

*When I asked the Lord, why this happened, this came to mind: I had been beating myself up about where I was on my journey. His response was, "Some detours you cause, and there are some detours I allow that have nothing to do with you. I am going to get you to your destination; there was nothing you could have done to change this night, but my plan in this, is so you can trust me."*

# DAY 19

## Fall in Love with Him

*"You shall love the LORD your God with all your heart and with all your soul and with all your might. These words, which I am commanding you today, shall be on your hearts."*

Deuteronomy 6:5-6

Love is the Supreme power of our existence.

God is Love and the *Authentic You*, yearns for His love. When you fully come to terms with this kind of love, it is impossible not to experience the truth of who you are, the Authentic YOU...

God expresses throughout His Word that we are to love Him with all of our heart. Whenever God keeps reminding us of something, it's because it is a Key to Life, a gateway to experience the deeper things of God; the true essence of our Creator.

Your soul understands this kind of love, believe it or not, and it desires to remember the **Journey with God**.

*"Love the LORD your God with all your heart and with all your soul and with all your strength."*
**~Deuteronomy 6:5**

When you love the Lord with all your heart and all your soul, then you discover YOU, the Authentic YOU and the God in YOU. Once you acknowledge who you are, then you walk in your purpose and who you were called to be. Taste and see that the Lord is good!

*"You, God, are my God, earnestly I seek you; I thirst for you, my whole being longs for you, in a dry and parched land where there is no water."* **~Psalm 63:1**

## JOURNEY LESSON

*I used to think I loved the Lord, until I began my journey.*

*I came to understand the true meaning of 1 John 4:19, "**We love Him because He first loved us.**" (NKJV)*

*What I discovered, is that there are no human words or feelings, which can really describe the love God truly has for me or you!*

*Until my Journey, I knew the Word said He loved us, but on the Journey to the Authentic me, nothing was hidden from me. Everything was explained in-depth. This is why seeking Him with all your heart and all your soul is so important. Because, Love equals More Love and it comes at you full force and overtakes you.*

*I fell in love with God and began to fully comprehend true intimacy; as this season with God was very intimate.*

*"For I am sure that neither death nor life, nor angels nor rulers, nor things present nor things to come, nor powers, nor height nor depth, nor anything else in all creation, will be able to separate us from the love of God in Christ Jesus our Lord." ~***Romans 8:37-39**

# DAY 20

---

## Ask. Seek. Knock.

*"For everyone who asks receives, and he who seeks finds, and to him who knocks it will be opened".*

~Matthew 7:7

What have you asked God for? What are you seeking? What doors do you need opened? Think back and remember, because you've asked for something in prayer; that's where it all began. The moment you set out in your heart to ask God, He heard you.

Jesus said that whatever you ask for when you pray, if you believe, you will have it (Mark 11:24). He also said that He calls you friend, and that everything the Father has told Him, He has made known to you (John 15:1).

When you ask, you have to ask from the core of your being, the *Authentic You.*

Flesh will try to make you doubt; however, this is the time you will need to let your authentic self-crucify your flesh, and allow it to have authority and power to do so in this season, because in this season the Lord will restore your soul to its rightful place.

*He refreshes my soul. He guides me along the right paths for his name's sake. ~Psalm 23:3*

Don't fight against it with your thinking. The best thing you can do is to let go and let God! And... stand in the truth of God's word (Matthew 21:22). Believe. When your soul seeks the truth, it will find it in God.

*For everyone who asks receives; he who seeks finds; and to him who knocks, the door will be opened.*
**~Matthew 7:8**

## JOURNEY LESSON

*Throughout my salvation, I often prayed to God and asked for an experience with him. I wanted more than just going to church on Sundays; I wanted to go behind the veil! I just believed that there was more to God than what I saw.*

*I wanted the deeper things of God.*

*Now, I had an awesome relationship with Jesus and loved my Daddy, but I knew there was more. When my journey began, as I have said several times, I thought I had done something wrong. Thankfully, God made it clear to me that I had done nothing wrong... that I had asked for this experience with Him.*

*As time went on, I began to comprehend what was happening, and I am now convinced that all who ask to be used by God and desire more of him will surely receive their desire. However, although there was a cost associated, it didn't matter to me... I was willing to let go. I was 40 years old and believed that God would not fail me.*

*I want to let you know that your faith has brought you to the Journey and Jesus is faithful to His Word. If you ask, you will receive, and it's a Journey of a lifetime!*

# DAY 21

## Your Ego Must Go!

*"You will keep him in perfect peace, whose mind is stayed on you: Because he trusts in you."*

~ Isaiah 26:3

The Merriam Webster definition of Ego: *The opinion you have about yourself.* It is synonymous with pride, self-esteem, self-regard, and self-respect.

The Journey to the *Authentic You* is a spiritual birthing process, and the Ego can sometimes serve as an enemy to your soul; therefore, before you can give birth to the true you, your ego will need to die. It's easily offended, needs to win, needs to be right, needs to be superior, and is always wanting more, etc.

The birthing process is considered painful, because these are deeply rooted and have to be plucked out of your soul. As your soul is awakened to the *Authentic You,* it will use its God given ability to purge these things.

When God calls for it to take the lead, it will move everything out its way. It starts with the ego, because once its fought that battle, then it can get your attention. One of the main reasons the ego must die is due to the reality that the enemy has mastered this part of you.

Once God begins His work, you are hidden in Him, and the enemy has been denied access!


**JOURNEY LESSON**

*This part of the journey may be one of the most difficult, because you have operated in it most of your life. It started as a child, when you were told that you were not pretty enough, or was overweight, or you're not good enough for the job etc. You begin to believe that lie.*

*I was used to being naturally able to make things happen. I was a born entrepreneur; business savvy, street smart, and strong in knowledge of the word of God. However, when I began my journey, it was one of the most fearful times in my life. To my surprise, none of it meant anything compared to knowing the Authentic me.*

*I didn't understand why nothing I did would worked. I tried and tried; growing increasingly tired in my efforts, until there came a realization that it was due to God doing a new thing, and that new thing was in the depth of my being (my soul). Flesh was not welcome on this journey.*

*He often brought the scripture to heart, that you cannot pour new wine into old wine skins. Instead, basically everything learned of the world had to die and everything learned moving forward was of God and taught by God. God wanted me to be a witness, and how can you be a witness if you have not seen anything before? This is where the following scripture that stayed in my spirit for years came to life: "Do not call to mind the former things, or ponder things of the past. Behold, I will do something new, now it will spring forth; will you not be aware of it? I will even make a roadway in the wilderness, Rivers in the desert".* **~Isaiah 43:18-19**

# DAY 22

## His Grace is all You Need

*"My grace is sufficient for you, for my power is made perfect in weakness."*

~2 Corinthians 12:9

The Journey to the *Authentic You* will have its days of pain; however, the pain is not to HURT you... the pain is to HEAL you.  It is when you are weak that the God in you can come forth. And when the God in you comes forth, you will walk in who you were created to be... the Authentic YOU!

Paul talks about a thorn that was placed in his side. We don't know what the thorn was, whether in his body or his spirit. Yet, like Paul, there is a thorn that's placed in your side, always nagging or pulling at you. At times, this may feel irritating and cause you to feel inadequate in your flesh.

Nevertheless, it is a gift to your soul. (2 Cor. 12:9)

There are Gifts along the journey that you will be invited to understand in God and His Kingdom. And you will later share them with others, because you are God's witness to the truth (Isaiah 43:10), and this truth will bring glory to His name! (2 Corinthians 12:7)

You may plead with God to take the thorn away. But that request will be a negative, because it is the very thing that will keep you. Therefore, when you go forth in whom you were called to be, you will not get puffed up. The thorn will serve as a reminder that without God you are nothing.... and with Him you have everything.

## JOURNEY LESSON

*I must say, this lesson right here was a tough one for me. And, to be honest, I still struggle with it a little bit today. Whether it is a speaking engagement, teaching a class, etc. I wrestle with the thorn in my side. It wasn't until one of my mentors shared with me that was a good thing, because it allows me to depend on the Holy Spirit to be the teacher.*

*I believed as a Women of God, a minister of His Word, I should not be feeling this way; that I should be confident. I felt that I should trust what the Lord gave me and know who I am. Instead, I was thinking about the fact that I didn't finish High school and I only had a GED, so how can I teach anyone anything? Looking at my marriage and how I failed, how could I minister to a married couple? You see where I would go?*

*It was frustrating.*

*Then, one day, The Lord showed me that this is the same type of thorn Paul struggled with; feeling inadequate and unqualified due to his past. He then reminded me of His response to Paul: "My grace is sufficient!*

*So, no matter which platform you may stand on, remember the feeling of 'not enough' is a humbling thorn. It's a reminder of God's Grace in the **Authentic You!***

# DAY 23

## Peace Be Still

*"And He arose, and rebuked the wind and said to the sea, 'Peace, be still.' And the wind died down and it became perfectly calm."*

~Mark 4:39

Think of a storm at sea. The wind is blowing, the waves are high, the visibility is zero and you're alone with girlfriends or your boys. So, it's like being in a classroom; looking to the front of the room for the teacher to explain the lesson.

Here is today's Lesson: there aren't any storms that will appear on your journey that God Himself did not allow to happen. The Journey is all about YOU and GOD. So, in this season, there is nothing that happens on your path that God does not permit.

If a situation (storm) breaks out, it is your faith being worked on and the Lord is yet showing you who He is. You are being asked to grow to the point that even when something suddenly comes against you, when you can't see ahead of you, to know that God is not going to allow you to drown. Thank Him for the lesson and ask Him to show you the blessing in the lesson; and then watch Him quiet the storm... commanding it to be still and showing you His will.

The Disciples learned this the hard way. The storm suddenly came upon them and all they could see was themselves going overboard. So, they cried out to Jesus, in fear, to save them (Mark 4:36).

And Jesus' response was, "Why are you so afraid? Do you still have no faith?" (Mark 4:40)

Trust the Lord to quiet the storms on your paths and there is no need to wake Him. God never sleeps, nor slumbers. He is watching everything and He's got YOU!

## JOURNEY LESSON

*There were many storms that came up on my journey, but God showed up as well. Every storm required my faith to trust Him a little more, and to believe beyond a shadow of a doubt, that he had me.*

*When I learned to rest in the midst of the storm, I noticed that He quickly silenced it; commanded peace to be still on my path. One of the greatest gifts that blessed my soul as I was discovering the Authentic me, was the Peace of God that surpassed all understanding.*

*This peace God desires to give us all. It is the only thing that will allow you to arrive safely to your destination in God.*

*I noticed that the enemy lost his power in this area of my life when I learned to rest in Gods peace; therefore, the havoc he tried to bring on my path was null and void, allowing me to continue my journey with absolute trust that God already knew everything I needed and that he was not going to allow the storms of life to overtake me.*

*I learned peace was a gift and to receive it knowing that the giver knows the reason why He gave it, and what and when I would need to use it.*

# DAY 24

## Strangers along the Way

*"Do not forget to show hospitality to strangers, for by so doing some people have shown hospitality to angels without knowing it."*

~Hebrew 13:2

Remember that your soul is on a journey; an experience with the Creator of Heaven and earth. Therefore, expect to experience things that are not of this world, but from the Kingdom of heaven. The Lord's Prayer says let it be done on earth, as it is in heaven.

On many occasions in the Bible, the Lord appeared, or put angels on the path of those He was leading.

- The three men who visited Abraham (Genesis 18:1-2)
- What about Jacob who wrestled with the man? (Genesis 32:24)
- Joshua and the battle of Jericho (Joshua 5:13-15)

The **Journey with God** is a spiritual Experience and will come with many blessings in disguise. You are on a path to discovering the *Authentic You*; therefore, the true you will be purposely guided along the journey and God provides for His own.

God puts angels on your path to make sure you stay on course. They are commanded to take charge over you to guard you in all your ways (Psalm 91:11).

# JOURNEY LESSON

*I often speak about some of the trying times of my journey; however, I can't leave out the strangers God placed on my path. The ones that blessed me were not my family, friends, or anyone I knew... they were complete strangers.*

*Those who were placed on my path to help, protect, deliver and heal, were often strangers I would have never imagined; like the homeless man who was a believer and I thought I was going to encourage him, only to receive a word of direction in my life from him. Or, the Manager of the office that I came to live in who was an Asian believer; I found myself avoiding her in the beginning, because I was late on my lease and I did not want to lie to her as to why. So one day, she asked if we could meet, even if it was just to pray. Now I surely couldn't avoid her, and I desperately needed prayer...*

*I told her things were changing, and to be honest, I don't know how, but I was on a journey and I was trusting God. These were her words, "You're right. You are on a journey and I will be with you every step of the way." What I didn't know at the time, was that she would be the one who allowed me and my children to stay there for over a year without paying rent. This grace could only come from God and the many angels that He commands on your path.*

# DAY 25

## God is Faithful

*"May God himself, the God of peace, sanctify you through and through. May your Whole spirit, soul and body be kept blameless at the coming of our Lord Jesus Christ."*

~1 Thessalonians 5:23-24

This journey is all about you and GOD. Beloved, it is a gift from God and He is calling you... the true you, the *Authentic You*! The one called before the foundation of the world.

Understand that when this call happens, it is not to be taken lightly. This journey is not the same calling as you were summoned to come out of the world when you first accepted Christ. This is the call of God to the God that dwells in you. It is His desire for us to connect back with him; in fact, it was predestined. (Ephesians 1:3-5)

The enemy will try to make it seem like, because you have not heard the journey taught or explained by your leaders or teachers, that God has forsaken you. That you're too deep, or that you have done something wrong, because you don't hear many people talking about it.

Don't be fooled, we are at the end of time. And, though many were called, few were chosen (Matthew 22:14). You are going through the journey because you accepted the invitation.

REJOICE!

When you answered the call and accepted the invitation, saying 'yes' to His will and 'yes' to His way, life as you may have known it changed. The change happened because God now fights your battles. If you have not gone through anything, you will.

However, you are not alone. The God who calls you is faithful, and you will be called His chosen, faithful follower (Revelation 17:14).

## JOURNEY LESSON

*I understand how one may feel when their journey first begins. The truth is that your journey began long before you noticed it; however, now that you have become aware, God is now ready to bring forth the Authentic YOU!*

*When I first became aware of it, I will tell you, like many others I was afraid. Because it's not as if God begins by telling you what's going to happen.*

*So, I was in the dark.*

*The best way I can describe it is, I could only see as far as my hand in front of me. I thought that I was going to lose it all, but I was reminded that whenever I felt this way, the reality was that I had already lost it all; what else was there to lose?*

*Many of you will feel this way, because of the uncertainty of this season. However, know that our God is faithful and He will watch over your soul. The enemy will not have access to that part of you. Our Lord will cover you with His wings; He will protect you, because you acknowledge His name. (Psalm 91:14-16)*

# DAY 26

*Lord, I'm Tired...*

*"Come to me, all you who are weary and burdened, and I will give you rest. Take my yoke upon you and learn from me, for I am gentle and humble in heart, and you will find rest for your souls."*

~Matthew 11:28-29

There will be times when you may often identify with the feeling of being tired. When we operate in our own strength, the natural effect is tiring.

So, in order to embark on this **Journey with God,** you will have to surrender from your work. You know... your plans, your will, and your fleshly desires. You will need to die to your flesh in order to travel with God.

You will have to surrender all.

God knows when you are truly tired, and it is His desire to teach you in the way you should go. The invitation to walk with Him doesn't go out before this feeling comes, because God knows you would not be willing to surrender your all.

Count all things with all joy; even being tired. Because anything tired must get rest. It's all in how you look at it!

Do you need rest?

Take a deep breath and repeat this: "God I thank you because anything that is tired needs rest. Lord, today I release every agenda that I may have for my life and I surrender it all to your will and to your way. Give rest to my soul, dear Lord that I may walk with you in your strength. In Jesus' name. Amen.

## JOURNEY LESSON

*I was tired! Almost daily, my prayer was, "Lord, I'm tired!"*

*As the owner of a business, I spent about eleven hours a day there; while having to transport children to football or basketball practice, go to bible study... you name it, I did it!*

*I remember thinking, there has to be more to it than this. I loved God, was saved, and trying my best to walk in the ways of Christ. I was trying very hard not to grow weary in well-doing. Nevertheless, the truth was, I had become tired. So, I asked God to strengthen and motivate me. My cry was," God, if you don't do it, nobody will."*

*It got to the point where I desired to spend less time in the office; I just wanted to be at home with my kids. Well, nothing could have told me that months later, God would answer me and I would lose it all.*

*See, God heard the cry from deep down in my soul and He is faithful. He is the Lover of your soul. He was positioning me to come to Him, where I would find rest for my soul. My journey began, and to my surprise, it would be a Journey with God of a lifetime.*

# DAY 27

## Lean Not to Your Own Understanding

*"Trust in the LORD with all your heart and do not lean on your own understanding. In all your ways acknowledge Him, and He will make your paths straight."*

~Proverbs 3:5

Do you know how much God loves you?

God is Alpha and Omega; He knows your end from the beginning. There is nothing about you He is not aware of and nothing can separate you from His love!

Do you trust Him?

On your Journey He is the compass that directs your path; if you follow the directions, you will reach your destination. And, on this Journey to the *Authentic You,* you may find yourself trying to figure out God's next move. However, God does not show us ahead on the journey, because He is trying to get you to trust in the Now. See, God does not live in yesterday or tomorrow; He lives in the Now. The Journey with God is all about what He is doing in you now! This is why nothing you have previously known works in this season.

It is normal to try to figure out what is happening in your life. You are fully aware that something is different; yet, as some already know and some will find out, you will not be able to figure it out. Why not? Because what God is doing in your life, He will only reveal in His timing.

The Word tells us the following:

*Trust in the Lord with all your heart and lean not on your own understanding; in all your ways submit to him, and he will make your paths straight.* ~**Prov. 3: 5-6**

If there were ever a time to trust the Lord, this is it.

## JOURNEY LESSON

*At the beginning of my journey, I tried hard to understand what God was doing in my life.*

*To my natural mind, it did not make sense. However, once I looked at things through the mind of Christ, then it made sense and I began to trust Him more. But, this took effort, and a daily reminder to lean not to my own understanding.*

*If I could encourage you in one thing, it would be to remind you that God is with you on this journey. If you make it your priority to acknowledge Him, in both the good and the bad, you can trust Him to make all the crooked paths straight.*

*What He is calling you to do, He also makes provision for. God's thoughts are not our thoughts and His ways are not our ways (Isaiah 55:8).*

# DAY 28

## He's Hiding You

*"He made my mouth like a sharpened sword, in the shadow of his hand he hid me; He made me into a polished arrow and concealed me in his quiver."*

~Isaiah 49:2

On this journey to the Authentic You, God will hide you. Why? Because He is protecting you, as He continues to develop you, for His purpose in the earth.

Sometimes, we think that since God has called us, it's time to move in the calling. However, there is a process to the purpose; refining must happen before we are released to truly walk in the purpose to which we have been called. So, as God prepares us, He protects us by hiding us.

This is a period of consecration with the Lord, and although it can be very isolating, it is in the isolation that we should be seeking God through prayer, His Word, and wise counsel.

There are some things needed to be pressed out of us, so that our oil is pure. He is setting us apart and preparing us to radiate His will in the earth.

*"He will cover you with his feathers,*
*and under his wings you will find refuge. His faithfulness*
*will be your shield and rampart. "* ~**Psalm 91:4**

# JOURNEY LESSON

*I remember asking the question, "How did I get here? Why am I here, living in the back of my office with my children?"*

*The Lord gently led me back to psalm 91, where He would share with me, that He was hiding me.*

*It's amazing how when your journey starts, scriptures that you've always read, will now serve a greater purpose in your life. This psalm was always my favorite, but I had no clue that He would use this particular one to encourage me in my darkest hours.*

*The Lord knows that what you will experience on your journey with Him is great. He is not going to let the world bombard you in this season; He will hide you from the cares of the world. I was in great debt, due to the loss of my office. Nevertheless, can I tell you, no bill collectors called me!*

*No one stressing me out!*

*I was up against a lot that could have wiped me out. BUT GOD! His grace kept me; it covered me and it will do the same for you! God's grace in this season will be a shield and he will not let anything harm you!*

# DAY 29

## Change Happens in the Midnight Hour

*"About three o'clock in the morning Jesus came toward them, walking on the water."*

~Matthew 14:25 NLT

Have you ever wondered why you are instantly able to get up between the hours of 3:00 -5:00 in the morning? The fourth watch of the morning is the time where the earth is still and the cares of the world have been silenced. Your households are still, and you can hear in the spirit, without distractions. This is the time where the Lord wants to be intimate and spend some one-on-one time with you.

Through the watch of the night the Authentic You communes with the Lord. This is the place where He reminds you who you are, and you find rest for your soul.

He shows you things to come and adjusts your spiritual lens, so that you can continue to see along the journey. You learn that this is the place where you can see the Lord and that you can trust Him with everything in you.

Call it spiritual boot camp, this is where your faith will be tested and will grow. This is where God turns everything that the enemy set out to do around.

Several times, in the Word of God, Jesus sent the Disciples away and dismissed the crowd. However, the full reason behind why He did this was so that He could be alone to pray. One time, the Disciples' boat drifted a considerable distance from the land. While in the fourth watch of the night, Jesus came walking up to them on water. In fear, they thought it was a ghost.

He then told them not to be afraid.

Immediately after this, Peter walked on water.

## JOURNEY LESSON

*Now, I had always awakened before 5 o'clock for years; without an alarm clock. It was my time to pray. However, during my Journey with God, I noticed that I was up at 2:30-6:00 in the morning.*

*I mean wide awake.*

*I remember the lessons in that hour, or the things that the Lord showed me the enemy was up to. But more than anything, I remember the time with the Lord; the intimacy. Those were some of the most precious moments along my* **Journey with God.**

*During these hours, the fourth watch, I had a strong desire to seek Him, whether it was reading my word, looking up words He put in my spirit, or praying. God was speaking like never before, and I was so in awe, that it reached a point that when I woke up, I ran to him.*

*Enjoy this part of the journey, for it is season you will never forget. Know that in the midnight hour, God will, and is able... to change things around!*

# DAY 30

## He is Near to the Matters of Your Heart

*"As for Hannah, she was speaking in her heart, only her lips were moving, but her voice was not heard."*

~1 Samuel 1:13

God lives inside you, and prayer is our line of communication with Him. So, when you ask from the core of your being (soul), your soul seeks the truth and finds the truth in God. It is God's desire that we ask Him questions; He wants to talk to us and answer us.

Everyone who asks... receives. God does not, and cannot, lie. While on your journey, you will come to understand that if you can think the question, God will answer you.

God gives us some examples in the Bible of what happens the moment you ask. It first starts with the question in your heart.

Let's walk and talk for a moment

When Abraham sent his servant to look for a wife for Isaac, he gave him specific instructions. The servant asked, "What if she doesn't come with me?" Abraham told him, God made him a promise and that the angel of the Lord would go ahead of him. When the servant got there, he kneeled down and prayed in his heart and before he opened his eyes, his prayer was answered.

What are you in need of my friend?

Ask God, seek His face, and bang on heaven's door!

## JOURNEY LESSON

*Many days along my journey, my soul was in anguish. This was because I had never experienced anything like it, and at times, the uncertainty was a little hard to bear. Again, living in the back of an office, with limited space and kids, things became overwhelming. I didn't want them to see me crying, so I would often pray and cry out to God from my heart. I began to realize that every time I prayed in this manner, my prayers were answered and had already been worked out.*

*When you pray from your heart things happen!*

*God's consistent reminder along my journey was that He loved me, and that He is concerned about the matters of my heart; wanting to heal every broken and wounded place that took up residence there. God tells us that He will give us the desires of our heart. However, in order to do that, we have to be mindful of the power of the heart and what desire means or looks like. One of the gifts of the **Journey with God** is that once we understand the matters of our heart, we will begin to understand the matters of God's heart... the Kingdom. Your heart is the greatest asset you have in this life, and in order to walk with God, He will come for it to truly dwell in it.*

*It is the door that truly connects us to heaven.*

# DAY 31

## The Soul Longs...

*"My soul longs for God, for the living God."*

~Psalm 42:2

The greatest pleasure of God was not in creating the flesh of Mankind, but rather the creation of the Spirit and Soul.

John 4:24 says, "God is a Spirit and His worshipers must worship in spirit and in truth." Your Soul, the *Authentic You*, longs to fellowship with its Creator. The Journey places you on the path to knowing true worship with God. It is an experience that you cannot be taught; only experienced, in TRUTH.

When you embark on this **Journey with God,** it is your authentic self, thirsting for Him (Psalm 42:2) and consumed with wanting more; not satisfied until it is filled. You will find this satisfaction in your intimate time with the Lord, in Spirit and in Truth. Your true self knows nothing else, so it yearns for fellowship with God. (Psalm 84:2)

Find that secret place with Him and you will find peace for your soul.

## JOURNEY LESSON

*Many days, I experienced this longing. It was different from my normal desire to worship and be in God's presence. This desire was from the depth of my soul. I wanted to experience and feel God in a way, like never before.*

*I would cry out constantly to God; not knowing why.*

Soon, I learned what David meant when he wrote, *"O God you are my God, earnestly I seek you; my soul thirsts for you, my body longs for you, in a dry and weary land where there is no water"* (Psalm 63:1).

That part of the journey gave me strength to endure all that was coming, as well as a peace that surpassed all understanding.

# DAY 32

## You Are Witnesses

*"You are my witnesses," declares the LORD, "and my servant whom I have chosen, so that you may know and believe me and understand that I am he."*

*Isaiah 43:10*

Beloved, you have been Redeemed!

I know the enemy may be telling you that you have failed because the Journey to the *Authentic You* has been uncomfortable, and he is trying to create an image in your mind that you have missed the mark, that you don't deserve to speak out and encourage others, and that you are not worthy.

But, that is a lie from the pit of hell.

Jesus sits on the Mercy seat for you and me. You are the very reflection of God's Mercy. Don't you dare feel inadequate or unworthy... you are the very vessel He chose to demonstrate His Grace, and your life has been preserved, not for you to keep quiet. Every bit of your life is a Gift from God and you are His light that cannot be hidden (Matthew 5:14).

The enemy wants you to feel insufficient, to keep you from speaking and declaring the goodness of the Lord; so that you won't let your light shine before men.

Don't be fooled! Rise up and take your rightful place. You are not just enough, you are MORE THAN ENOUGH. You are CHOSEN. You are God's WITNESS to declare who He is to a world of fear and darkness!

Therefore, your journey is to show you who God is, so that you can be a witness for the Kingdom of God. Let this truth ignite a flame and set fire to every fiber of your being!

Go forth with Boldness and be His witness.

## JOURNEY LESSON

*Many years ago, before my journey began, the Lord gave me today's scripture; reminding me that I am His witness. It was one of the scriptures which stuck with me, and brought joy to my soul, even though I had not yet come into a full understanding of what it meant. That's when this scripture comes to fulfillment.*

**"See, the former things have taken place, and new things I declare; before they spring into being I announce them to you."** *~Isaiah 42:9*

*Our journey does not present itself without the Lord first preparing us and telling us. He forewarned us long before it happened.*

*Thus, we are witness for God and in order to be a witness you have to see something happen. The* **Journey with God** *removes what the world taught you and reminds you who you are in the Kingdom; the Authentic You.*

*You will see many things on this journey, including your darkest hour. However, you will also see the work of your Creator, who is constantly showing you His greatness and power. Our purpose is to go out in the world and be the witness for God, so that others may know and believe that he is He!*

# DAY 33

## Don't be Discouraged

*"The LORD is the one who goes ahead of you; He will be with you. He will not fail you or forsake you. Do not fear or be dismayed."*

~Deuteronomy 31:8 NASB

I am aware that some of you may feel down and out, alone and forsaken; maybe rejected or violated, as if your joy has been sucked out of you.

Be encouraged and believe this... the world did not give you your life nor can they take it! But God is able!

Do remember the Promise:

*"The LORD himself goes before you and will be with you; he will never leave you nor forsake you. Do not be afraid; do not be discouraged."* ~Deuteronomy 31:9

This is a **Journey with God**! There is nothing new to Him; it has already been written in the book of life. It is new to you, and soon to be revealed to the *Authentic You.*

When your journey with God begins, the enemy does not have permission to your authentic self... That's why it is important to die to Self and not hold on, because in doing so, you give the enemy permission to hang around.

So, as the Lord spoke to Joshua, commanding him to not be afraid, this same word applies to us today:

*"Have I not commanded you?*
*Be strong and courageous. Do not be terrified; do not be discouraged, For the Lord your God will be with you wherever you go"* ~**Joshua 1:9**

## JOURNEY LESSON

*At times, you will feel discouraged, but that is when you have to remember the word of God and encourage yourself in it. When I found myself becoming discouraged, the Holy Spirit would remind me to "be Still and know that I am God" (Psalm 46:10).*

*In order to keep from drowning in pity, I had to remember to speak the word of God over myself. I held on to His **promises**, because the enemy will always entice you to look at the **problem**. Once you look at the problem, he will then encourage you to give up.*

*"And let us not be weary in well doing; for in due season we shall reap, if we faint not." ~**Galatians 6:9***

*Two of the greatest things that remained prevalent on my **Journey with God**, was His Word and His Holy Spirit. It brought me great joy!*

*So, don't be discouraged. His Word and His Spirit will be with you as well.*

# DAY 34

# Transition takes you to another Dimension

*"I know how great this makes you feel, even though you have to put up with every kind of aggravation in the meantime."*

~1 Peter 1:6-9

This season of discovering the *Authentic You*, may seem as if you have been in a prison, and the keys have been thrown away. But, I'm here to tell you that what appears to be a prison is God's way to another dimension.

On this **Journey with God**, look at the provision that He has already provided. He is there with you every step of the way. And remember His word at all times; it will keep you from the loneliness and isolation you may feel.

God never sleeps nor slumbers and there is nothing hidden from Him. He sees you and is well aware of your circumstances.

Continue to pray, continue to seek His face, continue to humble yourself before God (2 chronicles 7:14), and continue to believe that God is with you... despite the constant lie the enemy will try to speak to you. Instead, believe God's Word that says that you shall live and not die in the desert! You shall live and see the goodness of the Lord in the land of the living! You shall give birth to your God-given purpose and the Authentic YOU!

So that the authenticity of your faith—more precious than gold, which perishes even though refined by fire—may result in praise, glory, and honor at the revelation of Jesus Christ. When Jesus wraps this all up, it's your faith, not your gold that God will have on display as evidence of his victory. You never saw Him, yet you love him. You still don't see Him, yet you trust Him—with laughter and singing. Because you kept on believing, you'll get what you're looking forward to: total salvation. (1 Peter 7)

# JOURNEY LESSON

*There were times along the journey, when I was going through; however, I understood it was necessary and I could feel the Lord with me. The Holy Spirit revealing to me the process and that I have to go through it to come out as pure gold.*

*However, though it's a wonderful thing to feel the presence of God, what about when you don't? This kept me crying out to him. The enemy tried to use these moments to cause me to believe that God had left me.*

*Nevertheless, I held on to the promises that God had given me in the beginning: **I will never leave you nor forsake you!** In this season, I could not rely on what I felt. I knew that God loved me, and would not allow me to go through this journey with Him, only to drop me off because of bad decisions or choices. God is not like man... He does not change His mind.*

*Although it may not have been easy, eventually I arrived at a point on my **Journey with God**, where I could not deny that the presence of God was with me. Even in the darkest parts of my journey, God was there.*

*It may not have felt like it, but He was taking me to another dimension.*

# DAY 35

## Share with Others

*"Always be prepared to give an answer to everyone who asks you to give the reason for the hope that you have."*

~1 Peter 3:15

**This Journey with God** is yours and yours alone. No one can walk it for you. Many will question you, because they won't understand the choices you are making. This is due to the fact that along the journey, you will not make decisions as the world does, but as the Spirit leads you.

Nevertheless, do not be afraid to share with others your hope in the things of God. You are a witness for God, to share in His goodness and His faithfulness. At times, you will not understand the 'why'; however, you will submit to the process until it's revealed to you.

The truth is your hope is what's keeping you. Your hope is in believing what God is showing you. Your hope is in knowing that God will not fail you. Your hope is in the truth that those who hope in the Lord will never be disappointed.

Because it's a walk you have never experienced before, you may feel a little insecure at times, or you may feel that the only answer you are able to give to those who are asking *why*, is that "the Lord showed me" or "the Word says..."

Their response may cause you to feel uncomfortable, yet share the reason for your hope anyway. In this way, you will be a walking image of His Grace. So no matter how you feel about your journey, know that the hope you have equals healing, and healing equals freedom, for you and for others.

*I understand the uncertainty we feel when our journey first begins. The truth is, it starts long before we really notice it. But at the level where we recognize that it's happening, God is now ready to bring forth the Authentic You.*

*When I first became aware that I was on my **Journey with God**, like many others, I was afraid. It's not like God starts you off by telling you what's going to happen. So, I was in the dark. The best way I can describe it is that I could not see the hand in front of me.*

*My family and friends had many questions as to what I was going to do. The only answer that I could give them was, "God is going to work it out." Now, I meant that; I just did not know how or when. I only knew to trust God and had an assurance that all would be well.*

*It got to a point that I was not able to share the details with others' just the reason for why I hope.*

*Jesus always gave the reason for His hope in God. Many didn't believe Him, yet it did not stop Him. In the end, He was glorified, and at your end, trust and believe... so will you!*

# DAY 36

⁂

# Spiritual House-Cleaning

*"Because we have these promises, dear friends, let us cleanse ourselves from everything that can defile our body or spirit. And let us work toward complete holiness because we fear God."*

~2 Cor. 7:1

According to Merriam Webster, the definition of surrender is: To agree to stop fighting, hiding, resisting, etc., because you know that you will not win or succeed: To give the control or use of (something) to someone else: To allow something (such as a habit or desire) to influence or control you.

Everyone must go through the house-cleansing process. However, when you are going through this process, it will require complete surrender to our Father, so that your soul can be restored to its rightful place in Him.

The cleansing process means that everything once tucked away on a shelf, will have to surface, in order for you to make the decision whether to throw it out or keep it. Some of your findings will be happiness due to good memories, yet it may also bring up a lot of pain from those memories you had forgotten about.

Often times, we think of it as losing some things; such as friends, material possessions, or key relationships. However, these things are like old wine, and in order for God to fill us up with His new wine, a deep cleansing is necessary.

*"Neither do people pour new wine into old wineskins. If they do, the skins will burst; the wine will run out and the wineskins will be ruined. No, they pour new wine into new wineskins, and both are preserved."*
**~Matthew 9:17**

# JOURNEY LESSON

*To clean out my closet meant that I would have to surrender everything... if I were to ever receive the new and holiness. So, one of my requests to God before the journey really got started was, "Lord if I'm going to make it through to wherever this journey is leading me, please shut down the side of me that desires a man. And He did just that. I lost all desire as it related to male interaction; no breakfasts, lunches, or dinners. No phone conversations. Nothing! I was asleep in that area in every way.*

*Can we just keep it real?*

*In addition, there were other things that needed to be cleaned out of my life; such as, my use of Marijuana, telling half-truths, etc. The Lord truly wanted access to my heart; therefore, all of the junk that was hidden had to be dealt with. And, along with those other things, a male in this season would only be a source of contamination for me.*

*It was during this season of my **Journey with God** where I worked on cleaning out anything and everything that would interfere with my relationship with Him.*

# DAY 37

## Judge Nothing

*"Therefore judge nothing before the time, until the Lord comes, who will both bring to light the hidden things of darkness and reveal the counsels of the hearts. Then each one's praise will come from God."*

~ 1 Corinthians 4:5

During our **Journey with God**, it is normal to try and figure out what is happening; to make judgments on what we think.

However, as some of you already know and some of you will soon find out, you will not be able to figure out what God is doing in your life. The Word tells us not to lean to our own understanding (flesh), but if you acknowledge (Soul) God in all your ways, He will make your path straight. So, you can trust that He will reveal His plans in His timing.

*"For my thoughts are not your thoughts,*
*neither are your ways my ways," declares the LORD.*
**~Isaiah 55:8**

God is with you on your journey. His purpose is to make all the crooked paths straight. He wants to heal you and make you whole.

No, you're not crazy...

And yes, something is different!

Nevertheless, judging will only prevent you from moving forward. You truly have never walked this walk and if you judge it before its purpose is revealed, you will judge God, because He is the one directing it.

## JOURNEY LESSON

*One of the most important lessons for you to learn along your Journey to the **Authentic You** will be to stop trying to judge a matter. Initially, I was not even aware that I was doing so.*

*I remember being offended at my staff, for not checking on me, when the office closed down. I was hurt and felt used and abused. I had believed that as long as I was providing a source of income for them, they would be loyal; yet when I could no longer help them, they were on to the next best thing.*

*Well the Lord sure set me straight! One day, when I was scared and in my feelings, the Lord asked, "If you feel this way, how do you think they felt?" They had families to feed and were also afraid of not being able to meet their bills and becoming homeless. At that moment I had to repent of judging the situation. It was then when God was able to release me from that burden of feeling like a failure, and move me to the next level of my journey; then the healing process could continue.*

*Many of us do this and think that it's just giving an opinion. This is not wise, because our opinions are based on what we knew from past experiences, when what is happening to us now is something new!*

# DAY 38

## The Cost

*"The beginning of wisdom is this: Get wisdom. Though it cost all you have, get understanding."*

~Proverb 4:7

The **Journey with God** will cost you everything you know. Why? Because those things were learned from the world, even the church; and you will be coming into the knowledge that you are not of this world, but of a Kingdom.

If you are able to see the way, you won't need the spirit of God to show you. Everyone that went into the desert in the Bible was led by the Spirit. Most of them were hungry for 40 days; they were weak, they were lonely, but not alone. God said that He would never leave us nor forsake us.

Not having eaten for weeks will cause you to depend on God, and you will soon come to the realization that if you're going to make it out, it will not be due to your amazing survival tactics, but the hand of God!

Job knows better than anyone what it's like to lose something.  He lost everything... even his pride. See the pride (the ego) must go, because in order to walk with God, He must be able to lead. Therefore, the cost will be great, but the payout is even greater.

God never takes without giving.

He is not a thief!

Give it up and know that in order to gain your life, you must be willing to lose it, for the sake of the gospel.

## JOURNEY LESSON

*We always want to see the hand of God, as long as He doesn't touch our stuff. But, if you truly want to experience the **Authentic You**, LET IT GO!*

*Many times, I prayed for God to show me who He is, and to show me who I was. What I did not know is that it would cost me so much, including nearly all of my possessions!*

*You would think at this point, letting go would be easy, because throughout my life, I had always been required to let go of something; whether it was a relationship that wasn't working or a job where I knew there was something more out there for me. It didn't matter the cost, there would always be one.*

*However, I was finally at the point in my life where I was tired, and if I was going to making it to the point of writing this book, I surely needed Jesus to take the wheel and lead me to the Architect of my soul.*

*On your **Journey with God**, there is a cost to your 'Yes'. But the cost you pay compares to nothing that this earth could offer you. A walk with the almighty God is your reward.*

# DAY 39

## What You need is in Your House

*Elisha replied to her, "How can I help you? Tell me, what do you have in your house?" "Your servant has nothing there at all," she said, "except a small jar of olive oil."*

~2 King 4:2

This journey is about you and God and what you're in need of will be found in your house, God has already supplied for your need. Read the story in 2 King 2:4-7, which tells us about the widow who had lost her husband and was being pursued by his creditors for repayment of his debt. She went to the prophet Elisha and asked for help. Elisha asked her, "Tell me, what you have in your house?"

She had nothing but a little oil.

So, the Man of God told her to get her sons, go to the neighbors and ask for empty jars, and then come back in and close the door to fill them up. She did as she was instructed and the oil did not stop running until she ran out of jars. He then said go and pay your debt; you and your sons can live off the rest.

What is it that you need from God?

My follow-up question to you now is, "What's in your house?" No matter what the need is, on this **Journey with God**, He has already provided for you. Each one of us has a gift with in us; every one of us has an anointing. It is in the house of your *Authentic You,* and when you embrace your journey and go to the source to understand what it is, you will find out it's been there all along.

Oil represents the anointing, and it's about time you receive what's been lying dormant all along. What's in your House! Look around and don't look outside until you're instructed to do so.

It's in your hands!

## JOURNEY LESSON

*After losing my business, I reopened the same business a third time. When I still didn't succeed, I realized God was changing the course of my path and debt collection was no longer the way.*

*So, as I was questioning the Lord, I happened to glance at a candle on my desk that I had made four years earlier, which had sustained me and my children before.*

*I don't even remember why it was there. I'm sure the Lord brought it to my attention. However, my first thought was, "I have to go back to making candles? I have to go from making 15k a month to $15 a candle?" Nevertheless, I went straight to the storage unit and took out all my candle-making supplies.*

*The story of the widow and her oil became real for me. I came to understand that God was providing for me and that my provision was in my home. This gift God gave me in 2000 was the same resource that would supply my needs.*

*Whatever you need is in your house... look for it!*

# DAY 40

## Becoming Impregnated and Born again

*"You should not be surprised at my saying, you must be born again."*

~John 3:7

I know what you're thinking... born again?

Not just knowing Christ, but yes, born again.

Please understand, this is not about you coming to Christ again. This is about your soul; the *Authentic You!* Giving birth to your God-given purpose. And everyone who desires to know who they really are must be born again.

This Birth cannot be understood through human knowledge; it is experienced by God's Wisdom and Grace. It is a gift from God; a spiritual walk with Him who desires to show you who He really is and who you are in Him. This is not something the church or a school of Theology can teach you. This is revealed to you by the Spirit of God, so that you can understand the Kingdom of God. John 3:3

However, in order for this great **Journey with God** to begin, you must be born again. This rebirth will bring forth your authentic self and the purpose for which you've been called.

Embrace the process and rejoice in this new birth...
This **Journey with God**!

*"Jesus replied, "Very truly I tell you, no one can see the kingdom of God unless they are born again."*
**~John 3:3**

## JOURNEY LESSON

*Being born again does not mean that you do not know Christ, or that you are a baby Christian. In fact, the rebirth comes after you have known Christ. I do not want anyone to miss this walk with God. You must be born again in order to understand God's infinite Kingdom. The Journey is not how much you know about Church, it is an experience with the Authentic YOU, GOD and His KINGDOM.*

*The reason why you have to be born again is because the earthly wisdom you have gained up until your journey begins has no bearing on what God wants to reveal to you.*

*You have a purpose, and when you desire to know what it is, more than the things of this world, you will become impregnated with a process that only God could orchestrate. However, once you are birthed forth, you will never be the same; life will truly have new meaning. The* **Journey with God** *is a divine Gift and when you have experienced it, you have truly profited more than this earth could ever produce.*

# Just the Beginning

It's taken me almost 20 years to write this book. I wrestled with it, even up until the day of the release. Yet, it is not just my story; it is a nugget along your journey that will help you along your way. It is a journey of devotion that the Lord shared with me. Sometimes we have to endure so that others may not have to experience the path of despair; but, we all walk paths that need repair. So as God continues to give us direction in this life, let's add to our understanding, so that we can see the fruit of life that was pre-destined for us.

This devotional is not the full story of my life, rather a part of my journey, on my way to glory. I was given a choice, as will you, to accept the opportunity to walk with God. My answer was 'Yes', but little did I know it would be a gift that I would get to share with you; of the 'Godness' of our God, versus just His goodness!

Let me be honest, this journey has not been easy! There has been a lot of pain; however, I would not change it for nothing in the world!

Why not?

Because although I was once lost, it is through this **Journey with God** that I have been found.

You are also on a journey, my friends, and God is taking you from glory to Glory. You have a story, and it is my desire that both His Grace and His Love will lead you to the mountain top... and that you will *see the Lord in the land of the living*; marching in Victory of overcoming the world. May your **Journey with God** be so great, that you too will be able to share your story with others.

If you desire anything in life right now, desire to know God in a way that heals every fiber of your being. To know Him in a way that you understand every parable that Jesus spoke; desiring to understand His ways and His heart. This is what God is doing in these last days. If you have felt a tug that there is more, THERE IS MORE, and God wants to reveal it to you. You know the word of God... Now, let God show you HIS word by walking with you on your journey.

If you are reading this, know that you are more than a conqueror through Christ Jesus and that since you couldn't do anything to earn His Love, there is absolutely nothing you can do to lose it!

Beloved, NOTHING can separate you from His Love...

*For the LORD your God is living among you.
He is a mighty savior. He will take delight in you with
gladness. With his love, he will calm all your fears. He will
rejoice over you with joyful songs."*

~Zephaniah 3:17

**DHBonner Virtual Solutions LLC**
Editing | Cover Design | Interior Layout
www.dhbonner.net

www.ingramcontent.com/pod-product-compliance
Lightning Source LLC
Chambersburg PA
CBHW071125090426
42736CB00012B/2011